HOPE
WHEN ALL ELSE FAILS

by

PAULINE ROSE

ISBN: 1-903577-25-X

British Library Cataloguing Data
A catalogue record of this book is available from the British Library.

Distributed by New Wine Ministries
22 Arun Business Park, Bognor Regis, PO22 9SX
e-mail newwine@xalt.co.uk

Cover design by Elizabeth Ford
Used with her permission - acknowledged with thanks by the author

Sketches on pages 71 - 72 by Colin T. Hale
Used with his permission - acknowledged with thanks by the author

Edited by Joan Copeland

Printed in the USA

**Published by
Word for Life Trust,
The House of Bread, Ross Road,
Christchurch, Glos, GL16 7NS.
All enquiries to the publishers e-mail resources@wflt.org**

Pauline Ravenscroft (Rose)
aged 9 years

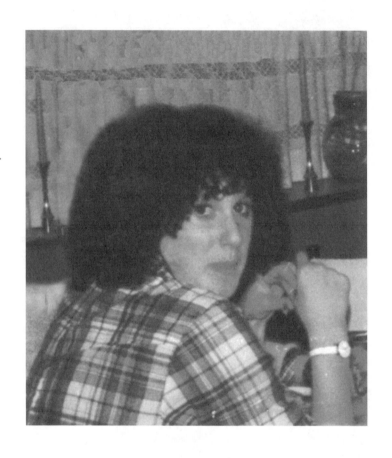

Jayne (Pauline's Daughter)
aged 17 years

Foreword
by the Rev'd Elizabeth Brazell,
Director of the Word for Life Trust

I had the privilege of meeting Pauline at the beginning of 2004 in her home town, Bideford, in Devon. She was attending a day called 'Picking Up the Pieces' which WFLT were leading for the local 'Cameo' group.

Pauline gave me a brief synopsis of her testimony and I commented, "You should write this down in a book, as it would bless so many others to hear of what the Lord Jesus has done in your life."

"I have already done so," replied Pauline. "I just need a publisher and someone to help with the proof reading, editing etc."

So that is where we started and here we are ready to publish at last!

May this true story encourage and bless you. It has moved me to tears and underwritten my understanding of God's presence in all circumstances. I have the great joy, and responsibility, of being mother to four adult children and now grandmother to eleven! Families can bring immense joy and immense pain, as we all know from our life experiences.

Pauline has been honest, forgiving, enduring and above all willing to give the glory to God for all the help, comfort and healing He has brought her over the years. If you would like to know more about the Christian faith, please do write to me at the address on the back cover. God bless you as you read on..............

(Elizabeth Brazell 14th February 2005).

With all my love to my precious
Jesus for never failing
to love and support me.
A special dedication to
my beloved daughter Jayne
who is now in glory.

To my family
for all their love and support
through very difficult times.
My son Michael, daughter Carol,
my daughter-in-law Candy,
David my son-in-law and my two
grandchildren Max and Freddy,
all of whom are
the love of my life.

Psalm 92 v 4
You thrill me, Lord, with all you have done for me!
I sing for joy because of what you have done.

CONTENTS

Chapter 1

CHILDHOOD

I want to share my testimony with you to tell of the many trials that I've been through and how my beloved Saviour Jesus has given me the strength to cope through them all. I'm not a scholar, writer or good with words, so this comes straight from my heart to you, with the help of the Holy Spirit to guide me.

Paul says in 1 Corinthians Chapter 2, *I didn't use lofty words and brilliant ideas ... my message was very plain,* and that's how I want this testimony to be as, above all, I want the name of Jesus to be glorified in all that I have been through because, if it wasn't for Jesus, I wouldn't be here now. As you read, I want your faith to be strengthened so that in every trial you will be able to trust the Lord more and more and, if you don't know Jesus, you will see that **there's hope when all else fails.**

I grew up in a non-Christian home. I didn't know Jesus and, apart from Religious Education at school, I wasn't that interested. I had enough problems to be going on with anyway.

My home life was, to say the least, very unstable. My father was quite often very violent. Mum worked long hours on the buses and I didn't see that much of her. I can't remember my mum ever cuddling me. Throughout the war years I was evacuated. I used to call the lady I lived with Mum, and my real mum Mrs. Wood.

I can only remember growing up in fear. I was quite often sexually abused and, because my mum wasn't there most of the time, she didn't know what was going on. My father was always messing about with me and quite often took me into the bath and into bed with him. I was also abused by other members of my family. My dad never slapped me; he always used his fist. I was terrified of him. The sexual abuse came often and I used to think that was the way life was, your father messing with you.

One day Mum and Dad had a massive row and Dad became quite violent. My brothers and I ran outside and stood looking through the window and watched as Dad beat my mum. He was bashing her head against the wall, her glasses broke, and I can remember crying out, "He's killing her, Dad is killing her." I was terrified; there was blood all over the wall.

I began to have terrible nightmares. I had no carpet on my bedroom floor, only floorboards. There was a settee in the corner of the room, nothing else. The light switch was quite a long way from my bed and it used to take me ages to pluck up courage to turn off the light and run across the floor to my bed. I quite often saw faces manifesting in front of me. I was so frightened of the dark. One night after I had gone to bed, my bedroom door opened and I saw what appeared to be a big ghostly figure coming across the floor. I started screaming in sheer terror, only to find that it was my brothers with a sheet over them. This was their idea of a joke, but it did nothing to help me with my fear, in fact it made it ten times worse.

One day my older brother tied me in a chair by my hands and feet and beat me with a steel ruler for two hours. I was seven years old! Then he tried to make me climb up the drainpipe into the bedroom window and threatened to beat me if I didn't do as he asked. He quite often had sex with me and had his way by making a promise that I would have a big doll. As a child, I didn't understand the implications of this.

9

One day I wanted to play a joke on my younger brother. I tried to find a drawing pin to put on the chair for him to sit on but I couldn't find one, so I used a knitting needle. He came and sat down and three inches of needle went into his bottom. I hadn't realised that what I had done could be so dangerous. He pulled the needle out, he was all right, but then all hell let loose. My father and my older brother came at me. I ran upstairs, slammed the bedroom door shut and locked it. I heard them coming up the stairs and then they started banging on the door threatening to beat me. I went completely hysterical and started screaming out of my bedroom window. Soon there was a gathering of neighbours, who did nothing but stand there with arms folded, looking up at me. I was terrified because I knew what my dad and my brother were capable of. This went on for several hours until my mum came home and released me.

My mum enrolled me in Betty Fox's dancing school, but I was always made fun of because I was so thin and tall for my age. We had to tap dance in pairs up the middle of the room and the teachers would literally be laughing at me. When the time came to be picked for a pantomime, I wasn't chosen and I felt completely rejected and I began to hate the way I looked. I did appear in a show though, at the Theatre Royal in Birmingham. We were being taken by car and several journeys had to be made to take us all over to the theatre. We were waiting for the car to return to pick us up, and were told that as the car was on its way back it had crashed, killing the husband of Betty Fox. It was a bad time but the show still went ahead.

My school days took me away from the family environment, but even at school I was bullied. One girl used to lie in wait for me and totally bully me; I was so scared of her. I used to be called the most awful names too. The self-hatred and insecurity in me really built up; I started striving to please people to win their approval. Believe me that never works. The phrase "sticks and stones may break your bones but names will never hurt you" is a lie from the enemy, because names do hurt.

My dad left us when I was about eleven years old. He'd apparently been seeing someone else and went to live with her. He tried to get custody of me, but my mum wouldn't allow it. Not long after he left, Mum put in for a move from our council house into a prefab and we moved in. I made some new friends. I never really wanted to grow up and you would quite often find me playing Cowboys and Indians at 15 years of age!

I sat for high school, and art school, but I was never clever enough. My brothers passed, but I never seemed to make it. I was always striving to fit in. One thing I was very good at though was high jump and I won several medals and certificates, and represented Birmingham. I wanted to continue with this and enrol in Birchfield Harriers but Mum couldn't afford it. I often wonder whether I would have taken part in the Olympics!

I had one or two boyfriends in my teens, but it never really worked out. Back in those days, if a boy even put his hand in the wrong place, he would have his face slapped. How times have changed!

I used to love to go dancing; rock and roll was my favourite. But one night, after leaving the dance to walk home, I was followed by a man who tried to pull me into the bushes. I was terrified as he tried to pull my clothes off. He stole my bag and I called out to people passing by to help me, but they just walked by. So I began to scream loudly and thankfully the man ran off. I was very shaken but I still had to continue on my way home by myself.

Looking back at my childhood, I can only really remember fear and unhappiness. I was sexually abused many times by various people and grew up feeling that's all I was good for. I wasn't accepted in love at all.

Many people with problems today have more than likely gone through a traumatic childhood, and if you are one of them, you need to know that only God can heal those deep wounds. He can heal you everywhere you hurt. Jesus is undoubtedly the best friend you will ever have. He's loving, kind, compassionate and caring. You can't change what's happened in your past, but God can change your future if you will allow Him to.

What amazes me are the words written in Psalm 139: *You watched me as I was being formed in utter seclusion ... you saw me before I was born. Every day of my life was recorded in your book.*
Oh, praise His glorious name!

Chapter 2

MARRIAGE

I met my future husband when I was 17 years old. I was with a friend at a carnival. We were both chasing after boys, as you do at that age, when I turned around and standing behind me was this really good looking guy. He winked at me and I was quite taken aback. The trouble was that my friend and I were after two RAF chaps at the time and this had come right out of the blue. However, I was whisked off onto the big wheel by this guy and he sat looking at me whilst the wheel went round, which made me feel rather embarrassed. My friend never spoke to me again because she had wanted him, but he chose me and that me feel quite special for once. He wanted to take me home on his motorbike, but Mum had always told me never to ride with strangers, so I made him walk me three miles home and then he had to walk back to fetch his bike.

After several months of going out together, the time came when he asked me to marry him and we made plans for our wedding. To cover the cost, I went to work as a clippie on the buses, just like my mum. At times I worked 75 hours a week. It was hard, but I raised enough money to pay for the wedding. Mum had also met someone else and was courting at the same time; we used to toss a coin to see who would have the settee! I was engaged at 18. My mum was broke, so I paid for her wedding as well as my own. At 19 years of age I was married.

The honeymoon was spent at the Pebble Ridge Hotel at Westward Ho! On the first morning when I opened the curtains, I saw a cricket pitch right outside the window. My husband was a very keen cricketer, so what did he do? He played cricket for the whole of our honeymoon and I was left alone. The rejection was terrible. I was a young wife already abandoned on my first day of married life, I just couldn't believe it. I'm absolutely certain that he knew when he booked the Pebble Ridge that there was a cricket pitch outside. One particular day I was so devastated that I walked and walked for hours crying my eyes out in sheer disappointment.

My marriage was far from happy; I don't want to go into too much detail because I've forgiven him now, and some of it's too painful to mention.

I didn't know too much about the birds and the bees as I'd never been taught. I was in Birmingham city just about to catch a bus when I felt really ill and knew I had to get to a toilet. Once inside, what looked to me like my liver dropped on the floor. I staggered out of the toilets and tried to find a policeman or someone to help me; I was terrified and thought I was going to die. I boarded the bus and all the way home I shook with fear. On arriving at my destination, I saw a doctor's surgery, which wasn't open, and started banging on the door; someone came to the door and I begged them to fetch me a doctor. There was a doctor there and he took me into his surgery and asked me what was wrong. I told him that my liver had dropped onto the floor. He replied, "My dear, if that was the case, you would be dead." Quite funny now, but not at the time. He then told me that I'd lost a baby. I went into total shock. I just couldn't believe that I was even pregnant. I had to walk a mile home. I telephoned my husband, who was playing cricket. He was most annoyed that I had called him off the pitch in the middle of a match and told me that he would be home at about 11 p.m. even though I'd told him that I'd lost a baby! When I arrived home my mother-in-law, whom we were living with, made me go straight to bed.

My husband came home at midnight! From then on I suffered

with anxiety attacks. I became afraid to go out and if I did I would have panic attacks. Many times I thought that I was going to die. I couldn't make my husband understand my feelings at all. I was a total doormat to him. Every day, I would have to put out all his clothes on the bed; I wouldn't dare put things in the wrong order.

We moved to Staffordshire to a place called Draycott and lived in a company house where, in 1960, my first beloved child was born. We kept a smallholding, a few chickens, ducks and guinea fowl. One day the guinea fowl escaped. I was nine months pregnant, and I went looking for them, but to no avail. I telephoned my husband at the office and was told in no uncertain terms that I was not to rest until I had found them. So, because I was afraid of him, I continued to search over the fields and wherever I thought they might be. Two days later I went into labour. My husband was playing football and I phoned to tell him to come home as I was having pains. He was quite angry that I had called him off the pitch to ask him to take me to hospital, so again I was abandoned. He did come home but he wasn't very pleased.

So my darling Jayne was born. She kind of crash landed and took a piece of skin off her little cheek. All the husbands turned up to see their wives and new babies, but not mine. He arrived after the ward was shut because he was on his way to cricket. It broke my heart.

I became pregnant again, but started to miscarry. I was taken into hospital and spent about four days in there. On the Sunday, my husband came to take me home. He'd left Jayne with a neighbour. On arriving home, there was no meal waiting for me, nothing in the cupboards to eat, the house was in a mess. He picked Jayne up from my neighbour, placed her on my lap, patted me on the head and said, "OK, see you later, I'm off to cricket." I sat and wept, I was so angry with him.

On January 1st 1963 my son was born at 7.30 a.m. It was one of the coldest winters on record, the outside of the house froze over and when you breathed in the air, you felt as if your very inside was freezing.

The midwife delivered my baby and then left. She hadn't even cleaned me up so I was lying in everything practically all day. I was totally alone, with a new-born baby, the room was cold and I cried my eyes out. By the time the nurse came in the early evening, I was still in tears and she was appalled at the mess I was in. Bless her, she washed me and cleaned me up and lit a lovely big fire.

We had a lodger and I still had to look after him. I had no one to wash my sheets or do washing of any kind, so three days after the birth of my baby I was carrying bags of washing up to the launderette. My husband refused to do this as he didn't think this was his job. The doctor was very angry. I also had Jayne to look after. I nearly fainted in the launderette I was so weak.

The cold winter brought disaster because my baby caught bronchial pneumonia. He was very poorly throughout the night. It was hard to keep the room warm. I had to phone for the doctor in the end and they sent an ambulance to take us to hospital. They kept him in for two weeks and I visited him regularly. He looked so helpless lying there. The nurses were brilliant and after two weeks he made a full recovery.

Life was so hard at home. I had two babies to care for and chickens and ducks to feed, with no support whatsoever from my other half, who was living a selfish life of either football, table tennis or cricket, so I was left to fend for myself again! I cannot tell you how many times I cried. My husband often went away on cricket tours for two weeks at a time, or played cricket nearly every day. Sometimes he would stay out all night and I never really knew where he was.

In 1964, my second daughter was born. I was at mum-in-law's in Birmingham for her birth because we were in the throes of moving to South Devon. It was an easy birth and mum-in-law was great at looking after us. My husband came to see us a couple of times. He'd already moved to South Devon with his job.

We found a lovely bungalow in Bere Alston, South Devon, and began to set up home there. My husband broke his leg playing football and they brought him home with a plaster cast up to his thigh. I now had three children to look after and an invalid husband, and boy, did he run me around! An ambulance came to fetch my husband to take him to hospital to check his cast and they tried to put him on a chair. Trouble was the man holding his broken leg went one way, and the other man with the chair went in the opposite direction. There was an almighty scream from my husband which sent my son into shock. From that day forward, my son started having asthma attacks and was really bad with them. Most summers were spent propped up in bed because he couldn't play outside. It was very hard bringing up three children on my own and coping with my son's illness.

By this time my nerves were in a really bad state; I would have panic attacks when I couldn't breathe. The nights were the worst and I became afraid even to go to bed. I lived in so much fear. I'd always been afraid of death and continually imagined I had every sort of illness. I believed I was about to die at a young age and leave my children behind with no one to look after them. I constantly lived at the doctor's and was prescribed endless tranquillisers, and because of this and the state of my nerves, my weight went down to seven stone.

I'm 5'9" tall, so I looked like a famine relief poster. The doctor got so fed up with seeing my face in his surgery every day that he eventually asked the vicar to call and see me. When the vicar arrived, he was wearing a long black gown and I honestly

17

thought he'd come to give me the last rites! For some reason, I had always associated vicars with death.

I never ever denied God, but I didn't know Him and I always thought that He wouldn't want to know me. I used to watch the people coming out of church on a Sunday all dressed in black, looking so miserable and I thought you had to be a special race of people to become Christians, so how could He want someone like me? Sometimes I would say a prayer to Him, but I never believed that He really took any notice.

We then moved to North Devon into a beautiful house. I spent many happy hours with my children on Croyde beach. We did everything together, except that one person was always missing, my husband. I was still suffering with panic attacks and lived on my nerves.

We used to entertain my husband's clients a lot and I would have to prepare dinner parties. I was left to do everything, and then insulted in company in many ways. He always referred to me as "the maid". I was working full time and having to run the home as well. I was verbally abused at work and then I would come home to more abuse. I then had to go to work the next day whilst he slept in. I was always having to cope with his drunkenness and insults.

My children went through infant, primary and secondary school and on to college, just ordinary everyday things that all families do. But the joy of seeing them pass exams and make something of their lives was such a thrill to me. They were a blessing and it was because of them I was able to survive my marriage.

I seemed to live in constant fear of death and just couldn't cope. My panic attacks increased and the doctor prescribed tranquillisers which I was taking three times each day. So that's how I coped with life really, trying to blot out things, sometimes not even wanting to live, but knowing that my children needed me.

With the children all at school my life was empty, so I decided to find a job and went to work as a temp in an agency. I enjoyed being at work, but working and running a home was very hard and I had no help from my husband. When I earned my first pay packet, he demanded it from me and gave me back some pocket money! We started to have holidays abroad, but he made me pay every penny and put my name on a clipboard crossing off the payments until I had paid in full. My holidays were terrible, he would get drunk and insult me in company and then find another woman he could try and charm.

My marriage was far from happy, and even though I tried my best to make it work, I couldn't. How I thank God for my children, the one blessing that came out of it all.

Chapter 3

JAYNE

Jayne left college and went to work in Denmark, where she taught English to the family she stayed with. She met and fell in love with a Danish boy, and they became engaged, but it didn't work out. It was whilst she was there that a lump developed in her face, and it grew to quite a size. She was taken to a dental surgeon, who removed it, but told Jayne to be sure to contact her doctor for a regular check-up when she arrived back in England. Jayne did go and see the doctor when she arrived back in England, but he told her that it wasn't anything to worry about and didn't ask to see her again.

Jayne recovered from the break up from her Danish fiancé, then she brought another young man home and we realized that she was in love.

I had always told my girls that if they ever got into any trouble to always come to me. I was devastated when I received a phone call at work from Jayne. She was phoning from hospital and was about to have an abortion. I went straight to the hospital to see her, but I couldn't persuade her not to go ahead. How I wept at her decision and more over the fact that she felt she couldn't come to me before and tell me she was pregnant. I would have had a part of her now.

That was another hurdle to get over, another heartbreak. Sometimes I wondered how many more?

When Jayne was 19 years of age, she started making plans for her wedding. I went to Plymouth to help her choose her wedding gown. She looked absolutely beautiful. We booked the hotel and church, and bought the bridesmaids' dresses. Everything was ready for the big day.

Jayne and her fiancée then went on holiday to Spain but when Jayne came back, she was concerned that the lump in her cheek had appeared again. I told her to go to the doctor straight away. When she came back, she told me that the doctor had told her that she was imagining it, and to go away and come back when she had something to show him.

Three months went by and the lump grew. Jayne went back to the doctor and he sent her to hospital. They operated and removed the lump, and sent her home with a tube in her face to drain the fluid away.

The lump grew again; I went back to the doctor's with Jayne this time and demanded they do something positive. The doctor said that he would write to the hospital, but I lost my temper and told him that I would take her to hospital myself. On arriving at the hospital on the Friday, we were told by the doctor that he was about to go on holiday for three weeks. He gave us a bottle of pain killers for Jayne to take until he arrived home and then he would see her.

By now the lump was so big that the doctor decided to send her back to Plymouth to have radiation treatment. That worked for a while, but then the lump grew again and this time more rapidly. We took her down to Plymouth again, where they operated and took out the lump. When we went to see her all her head was bandaged and she looked like a nun lying there. This, too, worked for a time but once again back it came, only bigger than ever.

Her face was so stretched I thought it would burst open. People were always staring at her when we went out and making fun of her. How cruel some people can be.

Whilst recovering from her first surgery, I began to call upon Jesus because I was so desperate. Jayne and I both felt the presence of God in her room; it was as if Jesus was standing at the head of her bed just watching over her. Jayne was reading a Bible, and the hospital chaplain was visiting her and praying with her. Then one day in my bedroom I called out to God to help me and I felt such a peace come into the room. It was wonderful, but I threatened God that if anything happened to Jayne I would never bother with Him again.

She came home for Christmas. Jayne was very ill but she made an effort to sit at the table with us on Christmas day. She couldn't eat properly because of the vile taste in her mouth from the cancer. We called the doctor in on Christmas afternoon and he took one look inside of her mouth and saw it was black with cancer. I was fighting back my tears so that she wouldn't see me cry. This was to be her last Christmas.

We took her back to Plymouth and they told us that they would have to operate again, only this time more major surgery than before which would mean taking half her face away. They would then graft pieces of skin from her legs to build up her face. I sat with her as they told her what they were going to do and I will never ever forget the look on her face. I went away and wept.

I went to Plymouth and stayed in a boarding house for three weeks so that I could be with Jayne every day. The operation lasted twelve hours. When I went to see Jayne in the recovery room she had tubes coming out of her everywhere. She looked so frail. They had cut away her forehead and taken out her cheek bone so all her face had caved in. There was a roll of skin like an elephant's trunk connected to her face from her leg. I just couldn't believe how hacked about she was. She was semiconscious and I took hold of her hand and said, "Hi darling." She said, "Hey Mum, they've taken my b***** teeth out."

The surgeon then took me into the hospital side room and told me that the cancer had spread to her lungs and there was nothing more they could do. She had, at the most, three months to live. I just couldn't believe it. I'd told God before (even though I didn't know Him) that if anything ever happened to Jayne, I would never forgive Him or have anything to do with Him again.

When I heard that she was going to die, I became very angry with God and felt that He had let me down and I wanted nothing more to do with Him. I started hitting the walls and calling Him every vile name I could think of. How could He be a God of love to allow this to happen? I just didn't want to know Him any more.

I then had to go back to the ward and face Jayne. She asked me why I was crying and I said, "Aren't I allowed tears of joy that I'm taking you home?" She just reached for my hand and squeezed it. My darling was so very brave and each time I had to fight back the tears because I didn't want her to see me cry. Oh, it was so hard, so very hard, to put on a brave face, knowing all the time that she was going to die. The journey home from Plymouth was a nightmare. I was in the deepest, darkest valley of grief and despair. I just wanted to die. Many people had been praying for Jayne to be healed and I really believed and trusted that God would heal her. I just couldn't believe that in three months I would lose my darling daughter.

We finally brought Jayne home, as I didn't want her to die in hospital but in her own family environment where she would have all the love, care and support that we could possibly give her. I slept in the bedroom with her and nursed her 24 hours a day. I became totally exhausted from nursing her, and watching her die was more than I could bear. I tried so hard to cope. I felt ill myself and even passed out one day on the kitchen floor.

Can you believe that my husband stepped over me and went upstairs!

I cried out to God again and asked Him to forgive me for calling Him names and said I needed strength to cope, and He answered my prayer because that's the kind of God He is!

Many people were praying for Jayne and for our family. All over the world prayers were being said. Even some nuns in Rome lit candles for her. People came and prayed at her bedside. One such person was a man of God who had a gift of healing and he spent hours praying for us.

On 7th March 1981 both Jayne and I gave our lives to Jesus. I was led to the Lord by my dear Vicar and his wife, and in the evening Jayne also made a commitment to God. She could hardly speak, but God heard every word.

Jayne was beginning to get worse though. She used many boxes of paper handkerchiefs to wipe away the continual pus that was coming out of her mouth. Her mouth had been stitched so tight that I couldn't get food into her or even tablets. We managed to get liquid in, but then the side of her face split open and the liquids started coming out of the side. She was sick from massive doses of chemotherapy and all her hair had fallen out. She was almost unrecognisable.

I used to wash her and hold her and tell her just how much I loved her and how special she was. She was always afraid I was going to leave her, even when I just went to the bathroom. She had seen her face in the mirror, which I had tried to prevent because she hardly had any face left. I remember her saying to me, "Mum, I will never look the same again, will I?" What could I say? I just took her frail body into my arms and held her so close to me and said, "I love you baby". On one occasion I helped her go to the bathroom and she started crying out, "Mum, I can't see, I can't see." That was the last time she was able to get out of bed.

It was so hard to watch her. I felt so helpless and I began to ask the Lord to take her home as I couldn't bear to see her suffer so much. She weighed about six stone and her weight was decreasing every day.

Then, the night before the 7th March, she started trying to rip her face away. She was quite hysterical and I had to send for the sister. They started giving her morphine. Her breathing became spasmodic, sometimes she would take a deep breath and I thought she had gone. I was crying so much and suddenly she opened her eyes and just said, "Mum."

The windows at both ends of the bedroom were open. There was no wind at all that night. Suddenly, she took one last breath. A whirlwind came through the window, across her body and out the other window and she'd gone. It was as if angels had taken her straight up to heaven.

The doctor came to issue the death certificate and I kept hitting him and saying, "Make her breathe, please make her breathe, she can't be gone, Oh, God, no." Next thing, he'd injected me and I don't remember any more.

When I awoke next morning, I jumped out of bed and rushed in to see Jayne, thinking that she was still alive. She was lying there so cold. I sat talking to her telling her how much I loved her and how precious she was, but she was so very cold. I just couldn't believe how cold she was, I wanted so much for her to open her eyes so that I could tell her how much I loved her but she just lay there so still. I had never seen a dead person before and it just didn't seem real somehow.

The nurses came to prepare Jayne. When I went back into the bedroom, Jayne was dressed in her wedding gown and was holding her bouquet, her veil was pulled over her face, and she looked so beautiful and so peaceful.

The undertakers arrived and I shall never forget how they put Jayne's precious body into a black bag and zipped it up. I felt as if they were putting her into a dustbin bag and I really freaked out. I was so hysterical that I insisted we follow the car all the way to Ilfracombe to the funeral parlour. It took me months to be healed of that vision. I used to have nightmares about it.

The day of the funeral came and I knew that people were praying for us. Endless flowers were arriving, the whole garden was covered in wreaths. We received hundreds of cards and letters. God gave us so much strength for that day. The church was packed, and I realised how much Jayne was loved by everyone.

I have never stopped thanking Jesus for all the strength and courage He gave us throughout all those long, dark painful months and for taking my beloved daughter to be with Him forever.

1 Thessalonians Chapter 4 v 13-18
And now, brothers and sisters, I want you to know what will happen to the Christians who have died so you will not be full of sorrow like people who have no hope. For since we believe that Jesus died and was raised to life again, we also believe that when Jesus comes, God will bring back with Jesus all the Christians who have died. I can tell you this directly from the Lord: We who are still living when the Lord returns will not rise to meet him ahead of those who are in their graves. For the Lord himself will come down from heaven with a commanding shout, with the call of the archangel, and with the trumpet call of God. First, all the Christians who have died will rise from their graves. Then, together with them, we who are still alive and remain on the earth will be caught up in the clouds to meet the Lord in the air and remain with him forever. So comfort and encourage each other with these words.

One day I shall see her again. Hallelujah!

Chapter 4

MARRIAGE BREAKDOWN

Not many years after my daughter went to glory, my marriage really began to fail. It had never been a great marriage right from the start. I was continually mentally abused, sexually abused and insulted, and I knew also that my husband was committing adultery. He wasn't a believer and his hatred of God was always aimed at me. His abuse came more frequently after his heavy bouts of drinking, and he drank often. I suppose I'd reached the point where I just couldn't take any more. I'd been married for thirty six years to a man who literally treated me like a doormat. My life was one of unhappiness and many tears. My three children were the only blessing to me through it all.

The time came for my son and daughter to leave for college. I shall never forget that Sunday when they both left at the same time. I thought my heart would break; to lose both of them on the same day was so very hard. My son bought me a record and I remember playing it over and over again and crying. They'd always been my life and now I was all alone to cope with my unloving husband. I cannot describe the emotions that I felt; it was as if a part of me had died.

I knew that God hated divorce, but the demons manifesting in my husband through drink were trying to destroy me. I knew that if something wasn't done, I would die, not because of my husband, but the evil working through him.

I was drifting off to sleep one night in my own bedroom (I'd stopped sleeping with my husband because of his abuse), when I was suddenly aware of my bedroom door opening. Everything appeared as if in slow motion. I saw a figure about three feet tall enter my room. It bounded across the floor, leapt up in the air, fell astride of me and, pulling the blankets over my face, tried to suffocate me.

I was terrified and called out, "JESUS, PLEASE HELP ME!" The figure then jumped off me and left the bedroom. It even closed the door! I just couldn't understand what had happened. I lay there in bed shaking from head to toe. On talking to my Pastor the next day, he told me that he believed it was a demon of murder who wanted to destroy me through my husband. I hadn't been a Christian long so it was all quite frightening. Each night after that, before I went to sleep, I covered myself and the whole room with the blood of Jesus. It used to take me ages to put the light off. I was so fearful, just like I was when I was a child.

As the weeks went by, the situation in my home became worse and I became desperate. One night I drove my car and parked in a lay-by and I cried out to God to help me. I cried from the depths of my very soul. The Lord spoke very clearly to me and told me to leave. It was the hardest decision I'd ever had to make. To walk away and leave everything, my home, and my security, but I had to do it. So I packed my bags on the Monday, aiming to leave the following weekend, but my husband ordered me to leave at that moment and started throwing my bags down the stairs. Oh, how it broke my heart. I felt so unloved and so rejected.

I went to stay with Christian friends. Over the days and nights I shed endless tears, I was so very lonely. I was 56 years old and had to begin my life again and I was so scared. I had no security, no money, nothing worldly, but I had Jesus, hallelujah! The strength He gave me was above and beyond anything I had ever experienced. Through the long lonely nights He would hold me and protect me and wipe away my tears. I stayed with my friends for about six months, but after that I felt it was time to move into a rented flat.

Before I left my husband, I'd asked him many times if he'd been seeing someone else. He flatly denied it. One night, however, at about 11 pm I drove my car past my matrimonial home and I saw a woman in there wearing slippers and dressed in night attire. I was so angry; I could have thrown a brick through the window. To think that he couldn't even tell me the truth, and to see another woman in what had been my home for 36 years was more than I could take. I felt betrayed and angry and my heart felt as if it had been pounded with a sledgehammer. I drove my car back to the flat. I drove at speed, and I had the urge to slam it into a brick wall. I could hardly see from the tears I was shedding.

When I arrived home, I was in so much despair I reached for a bottle of tablets and wanted to end my life. Praise God for His intervention because He burdened a Christian friend that something was wrong. She came round and sat and prayed with me. Looking back now, I'm not sure that I would have been brave enough to end my life; I believe it was more of a desperate cry for help.

My divorce came through within one year and I had the opportunity to buy a small house. I put in my offer and it was accepted. Two or three months went by and I was still waiting for my settlement to come through. My ex-husband was making it difficult for me to receive the money and kept delaying it. The owners of the house were graciously holding it for me and I was very excited. I really felt that my life was beginning to come back together again. I received a phone call to go and see my solicitor and my friend came with me.

When I arrived at the solicitor's office, I was told in a very cold manner by a secretary that I'd lost the house; it had been sold. I went into total shock. I felt as if I'd been hit by a bus. I don't remember driving my car back. My friend who was with me at the time told me long afterwards that my eyes were glazed and that I had totally switched off. She was quite scared. I can't say I blame her!

All I could think of was that I wanted to die.

I just couldn't take any more. I decided that when I arrived home, I was going to end my life and this time I meant it. I pulled up outside my friend's house to drop her off, and she told me to come in. I said, "No, I have things to do", meaning that I was planning to end my life. She snatched my car keys out of the ignition and dragged me into her house. I remember sitting in her chair and watching a clock on her television. Everything in me by then had totally closed down. My friend told me afterwards that she was frightened for me and didn't know what to do, so she telephoned another friend and asked her to come over. When my other friend arrived she told me that if I didn't snap out of it, she would take me to the hospital. I remember turning to her and saying so clearly, "I don't give a toss, I don't care any more, and I don't want to live any more." Next thing I remember was waking up in my friend's house. Praise the Lord, I'm still here, and praise God for caring Christians.

My divorce settlement came through. The Lord then found me a lovely flat and I moved in with the help of my Christian friends. I had some wonderful times in my flat; there were some great prayer meetings and many wonderful Christians came to stay who blessed me so much.

I was lonely at times, but I was learning to depend more and more upon Jesus. I used to sit on the settee and just hold His hand and talk and listen to Him as you would a friend. I did that from the first day I gave my life to Him and that's how I learned to hear His voice.

I went through times of having to be delivered and set free from so much garbage from the past. Much healing of the emotions occurred as I began a new life discovering who I was as a person and learning to love myself. I was still dealing with unforgiveness towards my husband and the woman he was living with but, with the Lord's help, and over a period of time, I was able to totally forgive them both.

Chapter 5

FORGIVENESS

The hardest thing for me to do was forgive. I'd been so hurt over the years, especially by my husband. Many times I just wanted to get even with him and make him suffer the way he had made me suffer. It was especially painful that he'd married another woman in my place.

I found this act of forgiveness a great challenge and many times I would say that I had forgiven him (sometimes even through gritted teeth), but the Lord knew that I hadn't forgiven. I was talking to a close friend about my husband, and looking for sympathy I suppose, when she turned to me and said, "You know, Pauline, Jesus loves your ex just as much as He loves you." This really spoke to my heart and was like a bolt from heaven to me. Who am I not to forgive, I thought. So with the Lord's help I forgave him. The freedom I received from this was wonderful. The hurts, anger, self pity and rage all disappeared when I learned of the love of Jesus and His forgiveness for me.

Matthew Chapter 6 v 14-15
If you forgive those who sin against you, your heavenly Father will forgive you. But if you refuse to forgive others, your Father will not forgive your sins.

When someone hurts you, you must forgive and release them, and pray God's blessing upon them. They cannot repay the debt they owe you for all the hurt and pain they have caused you. You cannot change your past, so why keep looking back? But Jesus can change your future if you will only trust Him.

You cannot expect God to forgive you if you won't forgive others. When you are in unforgiveness, the heavens will become as brass and God will not hear your prayers. So every time some one hurts you, it's **imperative** that you forgive them right away, and in that way your heart will be right before God. You will not go to heaven with unforgiveness in your heart. Another important issue is this, **you must forgive yourself.** It's surprising just how many people cannot do that, including myself at times.

In Matthew Chapter 18 v 21-35, Jesus tells the story of the unforgiving debtor. At the end of the chapter, the King was angry because the debtor wouldn't forgive his fellow servant, so the King sent the man to prison. Jesus says, *That's what my heavenly Father will do to you if you refuse to forgive your brothers and sisters in your heart.*

If we experience the grace of God, we will want to pass it on to others. When someone hurts you deeply, instead of giving them what they deserve, you must forgive them, even if that person doesn't repent. Forgiving them will free you from a heavy load of bitterness.

I cannot emphasise enough the importance of forgiveness. The Bible commands us to forgive others when they have wronged us. We must do this to follow the example of Jesus, who extends to us the ultimate pardon of forgiveness for our sins. Unforgiveness only leads to anger and resentment and can also be the cause of some illnesses.

Sometimes you don't need to go to the person who has hurt you, because they may not realise that they have done anything wrong. You could be sitting in church and, instead of praising God, your thoughts can turn to anger towards a person who maybe hasn't got a clue that they've hurt you. Total forgiveness is when you pray for your enemies and bless them, but if they don't forgive you, then that sin will be upon their own heart.

"Forgiveness is the key that unlocks the door of resentment and handcuffs of hate. It's the power that breaks the chains of bitterness and the shackles of selfishness."

Corrie Ten Boom.

I wanted to face my dad and forgive him. Thirty two years later, the Lord found my father and I was able to hug him and forgive him for abusing me as a child. When we met, we hugged each other and I forgave him. Three weeks later he died. How grateful I am to the Lord for bringing me and my father together. Later I was reconciled with one of my brothers and also able to forgive him.

My eldest brother came to visit me from Canada in October 2003 with his wife. I hadn't seen him since 1958 and had never met his wife. They were both terminally ill and, when he arrived, the first thing he said was, "Tell me about your God then." So I gave him my testimony. I was also able to forgive him for all that he'd done to me as a child.

In May 2004, my brother wrote to say that he was very ill, so I e-mailed him and told him again all about Jesus. I wrote two prayers, one of salvation and the other of forgiveness. I told him that he had a choice to make and that I wanted to see him in heaven one day. After he'd passed away, I asked the Lord whether my brother was in heaven. The Lord said, "You wrote the prayers, he said the prayers, so be assured, my child, your brother is in heaven with Me." Thank you Jesus!

If you want to show how much Jesus loves you, then forgive others. When Jesus was being crucified on the cross, He cried out, *"Father, forgive these people for they don't know what they are doing."* There were two criminals, one on each side of Him; one mocked, but the other asked for mercy.

So, how often does Jesus say that you should forgive?

70 times 7!

Perhaps you would like to say the following prayer of forgiveness:

"Lord, please help me as I struggle with forgiveness. Help me by giving me the strength I need to forgive those who have wronged me. I am sorry for the wrong that I have done in my own life and for the way I have hurt others and saddened you. Help me to make a new start in life and help me to know you better.   Amen"

SCRIPTURES ON FORGIVENESS

Matthew 18 v 21
Then Peter asked Jesus, *"Lord, how often should I forgive someone who sins against me? Seven times?" " No!" Jesus replied, "seventy times seven!"*

Mark 11 v 24-25
"Listen to me!" Jesus said, *"You can pray for anything, and if you believe, you will have it. But when you are praying, first forgive anyone you are holding a grudge against, so that your Father in heaven will forgive your sins, too."*

John 20 v 23

If you forgive anyone's sins they are forgiven. If you refuse to forgive them, they are unforgiven.

Ephesians 4 v 32

Be kind to each another, tender-hearted, forgiving one another, just as God through Christ has forgiven you.

Psalm 103 v 12

God *has removed our rebellious acts as far away from us as the east is from the west.*

1 Peter 4 v 8

Most important of all, continue to show deep love for each another, for love covers a multitude of sins.

Colossians 3 v 13

You must make allowances for each other's faults and forgive the person who offends you. Remember, the Lord forgave you, so you must forgive others.

You grieve God when you refuse to forgive. Because you've experienced His mercy for yourself, God expects you be merciful to others. When you refuse to be merciful, then you can no longer experience God's mercy. The measure you give is what you get back. So forgive and you will be forgiven. *God blesses those who are merciful for they will be shown mercy.*

Jesus was continually abused and rejected, yet in His love, He forgave and forgave and forgave. As Jesus was nailed to the cross he cried out, "Father forgive them for they know not what they do".

Chapter 6

MISSION TO THE ISLE OF WIGHT
April 2001

I began to be involved in missions at home and abroad in April 1993 with a trip to Romania. Travelling some 3,000 miles with two lorries, a minibus and a team of eleven, we took food, clothing and medical supplies to hospitals and orphanages. We handed out over 3,000 tracts, which we had translated into Romanian, on the streets.

In July 2000 I went as part of a team of ten to the Ukraine. A fifteen hour journey by Russian train was quite an experience to say the least! We saw incredible miracles of healing and many people received salvation. We held outreaches on the streets and shared our testimonies with many churches. It truly was an awesome time to see the power of God moving.

When I arrived on the Isle of Wight in April 2001 my host, a single Christian lady, shared how all the intercessors on the island had spent many weeks and hours in prayer walking, and had handed out thousands of leaflets in preparation for the forthcoming tent mission. We then retired to bed ready for an early start.

After helping to erect the marquee next morning, I was asked if I would oversee the intercessors during the mission. I was so thrilled, but a little apprehensive. I went back to join my host for lunch, tired and a bit dirty from helping with the preparations of the marquee, but a shower soon refreshed me.

The first prayer meeting lasted two hours and I was thrilled to see such unity between the people. The Lord told me that he has called this island the Isle of Fire! A Pastor asked me if I would lead the intercessors on Saturday from 10 a.m. until 6 p.m. and I was happy to accept.

After an early start on Saturday morning, the prayer and intercession began at 10 a.m. as arranged; three ladies arrived to pray. We had a separate tent from the main marquee specially for prayer so that we wouldn't be disturbed. During the day, other people came in and out of the tent to offer their prayers to God, but what impressed me the most were the three ladies who stayed all day. One lady was in her late seventies and two in their late sixties. What commitment!

Then we received a message that the witches on the island had been in contact with a member of the team to say that they were going to disrupt every meeting. We took authority in the name of Jesus and prayed that they would come to know Jesus. The following scripture was also quoted: *No weapon turned against you will succeed.* (Isaiah 54 v 17)

I was approached by our leader and asked if I would become the coordinator of intercession for all missions. All I could say was, "Praise God, Oh, thank you Jesus." I was ecstatic and I shared with a dear Christian brother my good news.

On Sunday the intercession began before the evening service. Some of the team were standing at the back of the main tent, when a young man walked in with his family and sat down. Someone who knew this young man told us that he used to be on fire for the Lord but had walked away because of work commitments. That evening the Holy Spirit was really moving and it was the one night that I was actually in the prayer tent alone, praying.

A brother came to me and asked me if I would pray for this young man to come back to Jesus, so I went into deep intercession. Later on, I was told this story:

After the worship, Jon came onto the stage and started to talk about the prodigal son. The marquee was only half full that night. About 500 people were present, but Jon was preaching to only one person and that was the young man mentioned above. Jon then prayed the believer's prayer after his talk and asked people to raise their hands. The young man raised his hand and Jon said, "I knew that you were coming tonight. I had prepared another sermon, but the Lord told me to talk on the prodigal son at the last minute." He then told everyone else to put their hands down for a moment as the Lord had a word for this young man. You can imagine the power of God at that moment. People started running to me in the prayer tent and shouting, "He's given his life to Jesus." I then ran into the marquee. The praise music started. I picked up a flag and began to dance in celebration. The Lord says this, "When one sinner gives his life to me there is rejoicing in heaven." I too wanted to dance with the angels in heaven and thank Jesus for all that He had done.

I was called to pray for two ladies who were suffering with manic depression. I laid my hands on them both and suddenly I began to feel a spirit of laughter bubbling up inside me and I remember saying to the Lord, "Jesus, this isn't the time or the place." Then the Lord answered and said, "Oh yes it is, for My ways are not your ways." So I let go and began to laugh and laugh and laugh and the spirit of laughter entered into the two ladies, who then went down on to the floor laughing their heads off and they were totally delivered of depression. Praise the Lord! The meeting then closed and I returned home to bed. Phew, what a night. Hallelujah!

After breakfast next day, I met up with the team for door to door evangelising. People we spoke to were still very angry over the war years. I felt such an overwhelming sadness for one man in particular who was blaming God for everything. The Lord told me to give him one of my books. In the road where he lived were many people who were angry and hurting and I went into deep travail for them right there in the street. We then witnessed around a car park and found that people were really seeking. One lady had a bad leg and we asked if we could pray for her. She wasn't willing at first, mainly I think because her husband was with her, but then agreed. So we laid hands on her and prayed healing in the name of Jesus.

I arrived back at the prayer tent and was thrilled to see nine intercessors. We started to pray and one of the brothers said something and started laughing. We were all holding hands and it was like an electric current going from person to person and the laughter became infectious and one person was hit so much by the anointing that he took off and landed on his back on the floor still laughing. Another brother tried holding on to the tent pole to stop himself from falling down; it was so funny to watch because he just slid down the pole and landed on the floor anyway.

Then stability returned and the service began. Not many attended, but five men gave their lives to Jesus, praise the Lord! As Jon was praying for the sick, I suddenly felt such an overwhelming grief come over me and I felt as if my heart had broken in two. Jon had asked counsellors to share any word of knowledge, but unfortunately for me, I didn't (shame on me). Then a lady came forward and shared that her heart was breaking and she received prayer.

After the meeting had finished, a member of the worship team whom I didn't know came over to me. He told me that the Lord was calling me out of the closet and sending me all over the world. He said that God was going to take me deeper into intercession and a mighty healing anointing would be upon me. Thank you, Jesus.

One morning in the prayer tent there were four of us praying and one brother prayed over me. He said, "Lord let the words be like wine to her lips and only the best wine, not Blue Nun." Well, that was it, I just fell about laughing and then the Holy Spirit took over and I was so drunk in the Spirit, I couldn't get up off the floor. I tried to crawl into the main tent for the start of the meeting, but my brother and sister just repeated, "Blue Nun," and away I went again.

A group of us went into Sandown to evangelise and decided to walk along the pier. We had to pass through an arcade of gambling machines and I was appalled to see fruit machines designed for small children. We walked to the end of the pier, then started to make our way back again. I was beginning to feel God's heart breaking and I began to run for the entrance. I just had to get out of that place. I left all the others behind and on reaching the street I fell on my knees against the railings and began to weep in deep travail. The promenade was very busy that day and many people were walking about. The team arrived outside just after me and some of them weren't sure what was going on. All I knew was that God was not pleased and I could feel His tears. It's a wonder that someone didn't call an ambulance! Afterwards I explained to the team what had happened but some of them already knew .

We had a couple of days' rest. On one of the days all of the team, possibly 12 or more, went on the train that runs along the sea front. Two had guitars and, as the train went along the road, we all sang praise songs and people were waving to us as we went by. It really was great.

I met two very dear friends called Ray and Vi whilst on mission. I felt as if I'd known them all of my life. We just seemed to gel together and we had so much fun and laughter. They returned home a week before me. It was during my last week of mission that I had the news that their beloved son Chris had been murdered and their other son Phil had been injured. We were all devastated; it truly was an awful end to what had been a great mission. It broke all of our hearts.

A couple of weeks after their son Chris was murdered, they telephoned me to ask if they could come and stay. Whilst they were in my house, a brother from Devon rang and asked my friends if they would share in church the next day. We agreed to pray about it.

That night the Lord not only told Ray and Vi that they would be speaking, but also that the church needed to hear about forgiveness. They also had a vision of a lady who needed to hear this message. Next morning at breakfast, Ray asked me if I knew of a lady in the church and described her to me. I told him that I wasn't sure.

We went to church and my friends shared about forgiveness. I was amazed at how much unforgiveness there was in the church. We arrived back home and the telephone rang. A Christian brother told us that, after we had left the church, a couple went forward and asked for counselling as the wife couldn't forgive her husband for how he had treated her over 24 years. After hearing the testimony from Ray and Vi about forgiving the people who had murdered their son, she wanted to forgive her husband. We enquired as to what she looked like and the description was the same that had been given in the vision mentioned above.

The Lord gave me the following scripture for my friends from Psalm 126 v 6, *They weep as they go to plant their seed, but they sing as they return with the harvest.* Many other people had the same scripture. The weeping would come when they buried their son, but rejoicing would come with the harvest. Ray and Vi went through the most terrible time, but their faith was strong and they had Jesus to hold on to.

They couldn't bury their son for months until after all the tests had been carried out. When the funeral finally arrived, I was privileged to be asked to read a poem which was a great honour for me. Their son Chris is now rejoicing in heaven and has probably met my Jayne by now. Oh, the joy of knowing that we shall see them again one day.

My friends are now in a ministry of forgiveness and have a web site set up: **www.forgivenessministries.com.** What was meant for evil, God turned around for good. Even to this day Ray and Vi are really good friends. They told me that it's because of the love I showed them by letting them stay with me that their ministry of forgiveness has now started. Just think, we first met in the Isle of Wight. Praise God!

Chapter 7

MY HEALING TESTIMONY

It all began in October 2001. I had a tooth extracted at the dentist and the socket had become infected, so I was put on antibiotics. About a week later, I had an uncomfortable feeling in my right side, so I made an appointment to see the doctor to have it checked out. After examining me, the doctor told me that it was nothing to worry about as sometimes the antibiotics kill the good cells as well as the bad and advised me to eat live yogurt. He told me, however, that if the symptoms continued I should make another appointment to see him.

I went to stay with my son and daughter-in-law in Sussex for a week and on the night before I was to return home to Devon, I didn't feel too well and the gripe in my left side had begun to be very uncomfortable. When I arrived home in Devon the next day, I was aware that the Lord was telling me to go to the doctor. The urgency of the Master's voice made me obey, so on the Monday morning I arrived at the surgery very early. I saw a lady doctor and explained what had been happening. She examined me and pressed all around the area that was tender but wasn't sure what was causing the problem. She arranged for me to have a blood test in the surgery straight away and rang the hospital for me to have a scan the next day. So on Tuesday morning I arrived at the hospital feeling very scared. During the scanning, I knew that there was something seriously wrong because they fetched a doctor and also rang my own doctor in Braunton.

I then became paralysed with fear and started crying and saying to the nurse, "I'm so scared." The nurse just couldn't console me at all. They arranged for me to see the surgeon the very next day. I have never ever been so frightened. It was bad enough going to the hospital anyway. Since losing Jayne I had become very frightened of hospitals. When I saw the surgeon, he told me that he would need to operate as soon as possible. When I asked him what was wrong, he said that he wouldn't know until he opened me up. I left the hospital totally devastated and so very frightened.

I had to wait for an appointment for my operation. In the meantime my church called a special night of prayer and people laid hands on me and prayed for my healing. Oh, how I thank the Lord for the prayers of the saints.

On Sunday 18th November, during praise and worship in church, I danced a dance of defiance towards Satan. It was the most expressive dance that I have ever done. No one in the church realised what the dance meant. On my way home, a white car overtook me. It seemed to be the whitest car that I had ever seen and in the back window in large letters it said "NO FEAR!" I am convinced that angels were in that car because after it had overtaken me I tried to catch up with it but I couldn't find any trace of the car. It had completely vanished!

The appointment for my operation came through for the 24th November, so I decided to prepare myself spiritually and began to meditate on the Bible. I looked up as many scriptures as possible on the peace of God and pinned them on my lounge door. I declared them over myself several times a day. In Isaiah chapter 53 v 5 it says, *He was beaten that we might have peace.* Every time I got scared I thought of that verse. I then looked up all the scriptures on healing and pinned these also on my doors around the flat and declared them several times a day and took communion.

The first thing I had to deal with was fear, because I believe that if you can be delivered from fear, then you can face anything. It's fear that causes the biggest problem.

A good description of fear is 'the darkroom where your negatives are developed', or **F**alse **E**vidence **A**ppearing **R**eal. *Fear not* appears 365 times in the Bible, that's one for each day of the year. God gives us special promises which, in times of fear and hardship, we can use like weapons to combat the enemy so that comfort, peace and courage will enter our hearts.

What will help us when all is dark? The knowledge that our Father is greater than anything. Just take the hand of Jesus to steady you, look down into the pit from which you've been redeemed and look up to the throne of God.

I said the following prayer many times:
> "Father, at those times when I am afraid, let me throw myself upon Your mercy. Give me the confidence of a shepherd who could say he feared no evil. Help me always to remember that the resurrection destroys the enemy's power to make me afraid. Thank you, Father, that Your perfect love casts out ALL FEAR in Jesus' name. Amen."

Sometimes, our world can be turned upside down through trials that all too often come into our lives, and one of the things that always comes with them is FEAR. If you can deal with that first, you will be able to face any problem or sickness with courage. If you are feeling afraid, please don't despair for there's someone who loves you very much and His name is Jesus. Trust Him and He will see you through.

Whatever trials come your way, if you know Jesus you don't have to be afraid of anything or anyone. So many people are afraid of death, but if you are saved you are guaranteed eternal life in heaven with Jesus Christ. Hallelujah!

Fear isn't from God, neither is sickness. Jesus doesn't put it upon us to teach us something. It isn't His will. If it were, then we are breaking the will of God by praying for people to get well.

Every day, before going into hospital, I declared the word of God over myself three times a day as my medicine. Proverbs 4 v 20: *Pay attention, my child, to what I say. Listen carefully. Don't lose sight of my words. Let them penetrate deep within your heart, for they bring life and radiant health to anyone who discovers their meaning.*

God wants you to receive your healing through faith in His Word. I do believe, however, that God sometimes allows us to go through trials to strengthen us. Look at Paul when he said, *Three different times I begged the Lord to take it away. Each time he said, "My gracious favour is all you need. My power works best in your weakness."* What about Job? Look how much he suffered. But God blessed Job in the second half of his life more than in the beginning.

Jesus became a curse for you; He bore every sickness and disease. When you are sick, declare that you are well. Keep declaring the Word of God over the sickness. Blessings and curses can come through your mouth. I never deny the symptoms, but I will not accept them as mine because when you say you have it, IT'S YOURS! Just imagine the postman coming to your door with a parcel. He asks you to sign for it and once you have put your signature to paper then the parcel belongs to you. I have heard many people say, for example, 'my headache', 'my rheumatism' etc. NO, it's not yours. Don't say those kind of things. Just say, "I'm not receiving this sickness and I rebuke it in the name of Jesus. Amen!"

I went into hospital with total peace in my heart because I had grounded myself in the Word of God and I knew that I was being covered in prayer. On the day before my operation, seventeen members of my church came into my room to pray for me. God was so wonderful, because He even arranged for me to have my own private room. I had previously asked the Lord if it would be possible and He answered my prayer. God is good all the time.

The night before my operation I slept so peacefully that, although they wanted to give me sleeping pills, I didn't need them because I knew that I was in the hands of God. I had His peace in my heart and His promise that He would never leave me nor forsake me.

Monday morning came and the nurses prepared me for the operating theatre. I remember being wheeled out of my room, but I don't remember any more. The surgeon who operated on me was a Christian and I was told afterwards there were also Christian nurses present. I often wondered if they played praise music whilst they were operating on me!

The Lord then said these words to me:

> "Beloved,
> I could have healed you before the operation, but you would never have lost your fear of hospitals and cancer. The fear came, my child, when you watched your dear daughter die. I have allowed this so that all fear would depart from you, for I have called you to be a warrior in my Kingdom and you cannot be a warrior if you are walking in fear. Beloved, you will come through this so strong. What doesn't destroy you will only make you stronger. No day lasts forever. This too shall pass. In the meantime, this trial will only drive you closer to Me and I will turn into good what was meant for evil. Be assured, my dear one, you will never ever have to go through anything like this again."

Then I began to understand, and I knew that the cancer had completely gone never to return and that the Lord had healed me. I declared Psalm 118 v 17 which says:
I will not die, but I will live to tell what the Lord has done.
Hallelujah!

The weekend came and the nurses were removing tubes from me which, I was informed, should have been in much longer. The nurses loved to come into my room and sit on my bed and talk. I shared about Jesus with them and gave them one of my books called, "Jesus Put a Song in My Heart." On Sunday, I felt so well that the doctor said I could go home, they were so amazed at my recovery.

So on Monday morning I was dressed and waiting for my son to arrive from Sussex. When he entered my room, he expected to see me propped up in bed looking deathly pallid, and instead there I was, coat on, face made up, hair in place and ready to go home. He was totally amazed.

Three days after I arrived home, the district nurse came to see me and talked to me about post-operative symptoms. She explained to me that I should expect depression, overwhelming tiredness and uncontrollable bowel movements. I waited for her to finish and then told her that as a child of God I don't have to receive any of those negative remarks, and I rebuked them all in the name of Jesus. I had NO side effects at all. Praise God! The day after the District Nurse called, the local GP called to see me. She rang my doorbell and, when I opened the door, was totally amazed that I was even out of bed. I was washed and fully dressed. She came into my lounge, sat down, took one look at me and said, "You don't need a doctor."

Don't tell God how big your mountain is; tell the mountain how big your God is! Amen! The mountain cannot grow any bigger, but you can.

"Father,

It is written that you will restore me to health and heal my wounds. You have promised to forgive my iniquities and heal all of my diseases. You said that if I would serve You, then You would take away sickness. You said that if I would attend to your words and keep them in my heart, they would bring life and health to my body. Jesus, You took my infirmity and You carried my diseases to the cross and if You bore them, Jesus, then I don't have to. You said that You would give me power over all the powers of darkness and that nothing would hurt me. Father, You are the Lord who heals me. I am redeemed from this sickness by the blood of the Lamb and I will not allow this sickness to reside in my body, so in the name of Jesus you have to flee from me as I resist you with the Word of God. I thank You, Father, that Your Word does what You want it to do and doesn't return to You void. I am going to walk in the truth bought by Your Son and the freedom that it brings to me.

I thank You, Father, for the cleansing, healing and deliverance that You have done in my life as I have called upon Your name. I prophesy and speak the Word of the living God. I command my body to come into line and the symptoms to go in the name of Jesus. Thank You that Your Word is Truth and that in Your name I have the victory. So I submit to You, Father, and I resist you devil, so flee in accordance with the Word of God and take the symptoms with you.   Amen!"

I went to church just before Christmas. It was only a matter of weeks since surgery and my Pastor had put flags there for me to dance with, but I told him that there was no way I could do it as I was still a bit weak. Well, the Holy Spirit had other ideas and halfway through the Praise, I found myself at the front with a flag and I danced a dance of victory for all that Jesus had done for me. The whole church erupted into Hallelujahs and Amens. I was absolutely flaked out when I had finished, but Oh, the joy of praising my Saviour for all that He had done for me. Then Jesus said to me, "*My power works best in your weakness.*"

The next mountain to overcome was chemotherapy. I was given the option as to whether or not to go ahead and I needed to seek the Lord about it. I felt the Lord telling me to have the chemotherapy and it was confirmed through another Christian,

Now let me say one thing before I continue. Some people who haven't believed that I've been healed by the Lord have said it was through the chemotherapy that I was healed, because if I believed that Jesus had healed me, then I didn't need to have any treatment. I sought the Lord on this and He showed me that although Shadrach, Meshach and Abednego were thrown into the fiery furnace, they were not harmed in any way. Also the Lord showed me Isaiah chapter 43: *When you walk through the fire of oppression, you will not be burned up; the flames will not consume you.*

So I had 30 weeks of chemo to face and it was not a happy prospect for me. I was very tearful about it, as it seemed such a long time to have to visit the hospital every week.

The Lord spoke again to me:

> "My child, it shall come to pass that your problem won't last long. Stay strong, go to the Word. It's all right, all is well. Lean on my promises. You are not going under for I am with you. Nothing living or dead, angelic or demonic, today, tomorrow, high or low, thinkable or unthinkable, absolutely nothing can separate you from my love for you, my child."

More encouraging words came from the Lord from Isaiah 43:

> "But now, Pauline, the Lord who created you says, do not be afraid for I have called you by name, you are mine.

51

When you go through deep waters and great trouble I will be with you. When you go through rivers of difficulty, you will not drown. When you go through the fire of oppression you will not be burned up. The flames will not consume you, for I am the Lord your God and you are precious to me and I love you. Be not afraid for I am with you and I will strengthen you and I will help you and I will uphold you with my victorious right hand. I am here to help you. Pauline, I will never fail you. I will never forsake you. I will never, no never, let you go, for I am with you always.

For I know the plans I have for you, they are plans for good and not for evil, to give you a future and a hope. All will be well. Let nothing disturb you; let nothing frighten you, all things pass. Beloved, I will meet all your needs. The best is yet to come. All is well, my child."

There were many times when I felt so ill from the effects of chemo and the smell made me feel very sick, but I stood on the promises of God and still declared His word over myself. All I could do after arriving home from the hospital after treatment was to lie on the settee. Sometimes, to be quite honest, I felt as if I was dying. I felt more ill from this than the actual operation, but I still kept on declaring the Word of God and took communion every day. On days that I felt so bad, I would hear Jesus say, "Dance for me." I would lift myself off the settee, play a praise tape and dance for my Jesus. The more I danced, the stronger I became and the more He filled me with joy and strength. The joy of the Lord is my strength. Amen!

Jesus gave me many opportunities to speak to people, and even when I couldn't, I would quietly pray for them. This, I believe, was the reason the Lord allowed me to go through the treatment, so that I could encourage and pray for others who had no hope and were fighting cancer. I gave out many copies of my poetry book, not only to patients, but to nurses and doctors. During my time of chemotherapy, I became involved in the hospital radio station and read many scriptures and poems over the air. It truly was a wonderful experience to share my testimony with those who were ill in hospital.

In March 2003, I went back to the hospital to have a colonoscopy to see if all was well. I was a little bit apprehensive as I didn't know what to expect. The Lord spoke to me the previous evening and said:

"Beloved, the future will be better by far than the past ever was. When you come through the fire, you will have a testimony so great to glorify my name. My grace is sufficient, I will give you what you need for today. That way, you must trust me for tomorrow. I call my sheep by name and I walk ahead of them and I have gone ahead of you, beloved, to arrange everything, so face tomorrow with confidence."

I spent the morning recuperating in the ward and the surgeon who had operated on me before came especially to my bed to tell me all was clear. Praise the Lord!

My surgeon wrote me a lovely letter to thank me for my book I had given to him:

"Dear Mrs. Ravenscroft,
A much belated but nevertheless sincere thank you for the very kind gift of your book. I had not been aware of the sad circumstances that led to its production and I was very moved by what you had written.
I know that your faith is obviously a central part of your life, as I think you know I try and make it mine too! It was a pleasure and a privilege to have looked after you and so it will remain! I know that there are some uncertainties ahead, but I also know that you will face them with your customary fortitude.
God bless you."

That was such a precious letter to me.

Many people today live in fear of cancer, they call it the big C, but I know a bigger, mightier and greater C and His name is Christ.

There is one thing you must do after receiving your healing and that is to continue to stand on the Word of God because Satan will try and tell you that you are not healed, but don't listen to his lies. When God says you are healed YOU ARE HEALED! Amen.

Chapter 8

HEAVENLY ENCOURAGEMENT

SCRIPTURES ON PEACE

I want to spend some time on this subject. As I mentioned before, if you can overcome fear, then you are halfway to winning the battle. Peace is the calming of internal conflicts. I daily declare the following scriptures over myself and they really have built up my faith.

Joshua 1 v 9
I command you - be strong and courageous!
Do not be afraid or discouraged
For the Lord your God is with you wherever you go.

Exodus 14 v 13
Don't be afraid.
Just stand where you are and watch the Lord rescue you.

Deuteronomy 20 v 1
Do not be afraid. The Lord your God ... is with you.

Nehemiah 8 v 10

Don't be dejected and sad, for the joy of the Lord is your strength!

Psalm 23 v 4

Even when I walk through the dark valley of death, I will not be afraid.

Psalm 27 v 1-2

The Lord is my light and salvation - so why should I be afraid?

Psalm 34 v 4

I prayed to the Lord, and he answered me, freeing me from all my fears.

Psalm 49 v 5

There is no need to fear when times of trouble come.

Psalm 56 v 3

When I am afraid, I put my trust in you.

Psalm 57 v 1

I will hide beneath the shadow of your wings until this violent storm is past.

Psalm 62 v 6

He alone is my rock and my salvation, my fortress where I will not be shaken.

Isaiah 26 v 3

You will keep in perfect peace all who trust in you, whose thoughts are fixed on you!

Isaiah 41 v 10

Don't be afraid, for I am with you.

Isaiah 44 v 6-8
I am the First and the Last; there is no other God. ...
Do not tremble; do not be afraid.

Isaiah 54 v 14
You will live under a government that is just and fair. Your
enemies will stay far away; you will live in peace. Terror will
not come near.

Jeremiah 17 v 7-8
Blessed are those who trust in the Lord and who have made the
Lord their hope and confidence. They are like trees planted
along a riverbank, with roots that reach deep into the water.
Such trees are not bothered by the heat or worried by long
months of drought. Their leaves stay green, and they go right
on producing delicious fruit.

John 14 v 27
I am leaving you with a gift - peace of mind and heart.
And the peace I give isn't like the peace the world gives.
So don't be troubled or afraid.

2 Timothy 1 v 7
For God has not given us a spirit of fear and timidity.
but of power, love, and self-discipline.

1 John 4 v 18
Such love has no fear because perfect love expels all fear.

"You, Satan, will obey the word of the resurrected Son of the living God who said, 'Behold I give you power over all the enemy and in my name you shall have authority. You shall cast out all evil.'

So, you foul spirit of fear, you do not come from God. I identify you because it is written that God has not given me a spirit of fear, but of love, power and a sound mind. I bind you, work of fear, you controlling power, you dominating spirit, you lying, influencing work of the enemy. In the name of Jesus be bound over the control of my mind. Be bound over the control of my spirit. In the name of Jesus be bound now, your power is broken, your spirit is broken, and he whom the Son sets free is free indeed. Amen"

Fear is a sin; a person who fears says in effect, "I cannot trust God to work it out, so I will take matters into my own hands." What then is the result? Worry and fear. With God, however, you can meet it, face it and overcome it.

Ask yourself this, what is there to fear? The past is under His blood, the present is protected by His power, and the future is provided and prepared for by His grace.

Worry and fear are the advance interest you pay on your troubles that might never come. When you take one day at a time, you will be able to draw from the bank of God's grace sufficient to meet every bill that life claims from you. If, however, you borrow from tomorrow's troubles, then you won't have enough to pay your bills.

If you walk closely with Jesus day by day, you will so cultivate and practise the presence of God that, when fears or anxieties arise, you will be prepared and in such loving fellowship with Him that you will find complete deliverance. Stand fast, therefore, in the freedom in which Christ has set you free.

Submit yourself to God and remember that God has not given you a spirit of fear.

What are you afraid of? Don't you know that your Father is with you? Every step you take He is with you. If you fall, He will pick you up. If you walk with Him, He will guarantee that you will reach your destiny. You are so special in His eyes; He loves you and cherishes you so much. Today, beloved, rest in His love, feel His strength and His presence and begin to move ahead without fear.

Then Jesus got into the boat and started across the lake with his disciples. Suddenly, a terrible storm came up, with waves breaking into the boat. But Jesus was sleeping. The disciples went to him and woke him up shouting, "Lord, save us! We're going to drown!" And Jesus answered, "Why are you afraid? You have so little faith!" Then he stood up and rebuked the wind and waves, and suddenly all was calm. (Matthew Chapter 8 v 23)

Remember, when the storms of life come, and they do, that no matter how fierce the storm may rage, Jesus is in the boat with you.

Storms of Life

When storms of life come crowding in
As they so often do,
Trust the Lord, have faith in him
And he will see you through.

When wind and waves surround you,
And life brings sorrow or pain,
Jesus will still the raging storm
And restore your peace again.

He'll calm the troubled waters,
The storms of life will cease,
If you will keep your eyes on him,
You will know his joy and peace.

He will never, never leave you
To face the storm alone,
He'll gently whisper, "Peace be still,"
And bring you safely home.

So always keep your eyes on him
And never ever fear,
Though skies are grey and storms may rage,
The Lord is always near.

SCRIPTURES ON HEALING

God wants you to receive your healing through faith in His Word. He wants you to confess the Word and be healed, for the Word is health to your flesh. Don't concentrate on your sickness, but allow the Word of God to penetrate deep into your heart and spirit.

Proverbs 4 v 20-22
Pay attention, my child, to what I say. Listen carefully. Don't lose sight of my words. Let them penetrate deep within your heart, for they bring life and radiant health to anyone who discovers their meaning.

Exodus 15 v 26
I am the Lord who heals you.

Psalm 41 v 3
The Lord nurses them when they are sick, and eases their pain and discomfort.

Psalm 91 v 10-11
No evil will conquer you; no plague will come near your dwelling.

Psalm 103 v 2-5
Praise the Lord, I tell myself, and never forget the good things he does for me. He forgives all my sins and heals all my diseases. He ransoms me from death and surrounds me with love and tender mercies. He fills my life with good things. My youth is renewed like the eagle's.

Psalm 118 v 17
I will not die, but I will live to tell what the Lord has done.

Isaiah 58 v 8
Your healing will come quickly.

Proverbs 12 v 28
The way of the godly leads to life;
their path does not lead to death.

Jeremiah 17 v 14
Oh Lord, you alone can heal me; you alone can save.
My praises are for you alone!

Jeremiah 29 v 11
For I know the plans I have for you, ... they are plans for good
and not for disaster, to give you a future and a hope.

Jeremiah 30 v 17
I will give you back your health and heal your wounds.

Matthew 15 v 13
Every plant not planted by my heavenly Father will be rooted
up.

John 6 v 63
The very words that I have spoken to you are spirit and life.

1 Corinthians 6 v 13
Our bodies ... were made for the Lord,
and the Lord cares about our bodies.

1 Corinthians 6 v 19
Your body is the temple of the Holy Spirit.

James 5 v 15
Their prayer offered in faith will save the sick
and the Lord will make them well.

1 Peter 2 v 24
He personally carried away our sins in his own body on the
cross so we can be dead to sin and live for what is right.
You have been healed by his wounds!

I John 4 v 4
The Spirit who lives in you
is greater than the spirit who lives in the world.

God blesses the people who patiently endure testing, because when they have stood the test, they will receive the crown of life that God has promised to those who love Him.

The devil has no place in me, no power over me, no unsettled claims against me. ALL has been settled by the blood of Jesus.

Sometimes after a time of prayer for healing, you may find yourself disappointed as the symptoms still appear to persist. You know that you have received your healing, but you need to realise that the enemy doesn't want to let you go. He will try to persuade you that you are not healed and that's why you have the symptoms. Remember he is a liar and the father of all lies. Jesus is stronger, so tell the devil to GO IN JESUS' NAME. Amen!

A LOVE LETTER TO JESUS

Dearest Jesus,

With all my heart I will sing your praises and give thanks to your name for your unfailing love and faithfulness, because all your promises are backed by all the honour of your name. When I pray, you answer me; you encourage me by giving me the strength I need.

Lord, I know that if it wasn't for you, I wouldn't be here today. I know that I sometimes break your heart and yet, oh Lord, you still love me. I cannot explain this kind of love, this kind of grace.

Lord, I love the way you hold me close and tell me how much you love me. I love the way you laugh when I'm happy and cry when I'm sad. I love the way you carry me in your arms when I feel I can't go on. I love your faithfulness. I love the gentle way you take my hand and lead me. Oh, Jesus, I just love everything about you. I never knew what true love was until I met you.

You are everything that is love to me. You are my strength and my shield. My cup continually overflows with your blessings. You have restored my health, and you have thrilled me with all that you have done for me. No wonder that my heart is filled with so much joy. You have turned my mourning into dancing, and my sorrow into joy.

I love you Lord with all my heart,

Pauline Rose

LETTER FROM THE FATHER
TAKEN FROM EPHESIANS

My child,

I have blessed you with every spiritual blessing in the heavenly places because you belong to me. Long ago, before I made the world, I loved you and chose you in Christ to be holy and without fault. My unchanging plan has always been to adopt you into my family by bringing you to myself through my Son, Jesus and this has given me great pleasure.

My secret plan has now been revealed to you. It's a plan centred on my Son, Jesus, designed long ago according to my great pleasure. And this is my plan. At the right time I will bring everything together under the authority of Jesus, everything in heaven and on earth. For I chose you from the beginning and all things have happened just as I, the Lord your God, decided long ago. Now you have heard the truth and believed in Christ. He has identified you as his own by giving you the Holy Spirit, whom he promised long ago. The Spirit is my guarantee that I will give you everything I promised and that I have purchased you to be my own.

I love you so very much that, even when you were dead because of your sins, I gave you life when I raised my Son from the dead. For I raised you from the dead along with Christ and you are seated with him in the heavenly realms. Now you belong to Christ Jesus. Though you were far away from me, now you have been brought near because of the blood of my Son. Now you are a member of my family, for I created everything in heaven and on earth.

I want you to grow in the knowledge of your God. I want your heart to be flooded with light so that you will understand the wonderful future I have promised you. I want you to realise what a rich and glorious inheritance I have given to you. I want you to understand the incredible greatness of my power. This is the same mighty power that raised my Son from the dead, and now he is seated in the place of honour at my right hand in the heavenly realms.

I saved you by my special favour when you believed. You are my masterpiece and I have created you anew in Christ Jesus. From my glorious unlimited resources I will give you mighty inner strength through my Holy Spirit.

Throw off your old evil nature and your former way of life. Instead there must be a spiritual renewal of your thoughts and attitudes. You must display a new nature because you are a new person created in my likeness, righteous and true. Follow my example in everything you do because you are my dear child. Live a life filled with love for others, following the example of my beloved Son who gave himself as a sacrifice to take away your sins. I was pleased because that sacrifice was like sweet perfume to me

I want your roots to go down deep into the soil of my love and I want you to have the power to understand, beloved, just how much your Father in heaven loves you. I want you to know how wide, how long and how deep my love is for you and to experience my love, though it's so great that you will never fully understand it. Then you will be filled with the fullness of life and power that comes from me.

Be careful, beloved, how you live. Make the most of every opportunity for doing good in these evil days. Don't act thoughtlessly, but try and understand what I want you to do. Let my Holy Spirit fill and control you.

One final word, be strong with my mighty power, put on all of the armour so that you will be able to stand firm, for you are not fighting against flesh and blood, but against the evil rulers and authorities of the unseen world.

Use every piece of the armour I have given to you to resist the enemy, so that after the battle you will still be standing. Pray at all times and on every occasion. Stay alert and be persistent in your prayers.

May grace and peace be yours forever and ever.

Your loving Heavenly Father

RACE TRACKS

I saw a picture of a racetrack and people were running round and round it, jumping over the same hurdles. They were just constantly going round in circles. I then saw an open gate and the Lord spoke the following words:

"My dear ones,
I want you to stop running round and round this track and jumping over the same hurdles. I'm calling you to go through the gate that I have opened for you, a gate that no man can shut. And run, run as if in a marathon. I'm calling you to go out into the highways and byways where the people are, and run the race that I have set before you, a race that starts and finishes.

Beloved, throw off everything that hinders you and keeps you from the truth of my word and run with perseverance the race that I have set before you. Run straight to the goal with purpose in every step. Look straight ahead and fix your eyes on what lies ahead. Do not look back from whence you came. Run and run to win, and keep on keeping on. When you become tired or discouraged, fear not, for I will refresh you, I will encourage you. Do not allow the enemy to take you back into situations where I have set you free, for whom the Son sets free is free indeed. The enemy will rob you of everything if you allow him to. He will have you running round in circles and jumping over the same old hurdles. Beloved, break free, for I have truly set you free to run the race that I have set before you, and receive the eternal prize that I have for each one of you. Remember I am with you always and that I love you."

Go Through the Gate I Have Opened for You

The second racetrack the Lord showed me was a straight one. There were obstacles and barriers to overcome, but people were dealing with the hurdles. They were jumping over them and running hard to win. The track was lined with angels who were cheering them on and shouting, "Come on, you can make it!" From the grandstand came the cheers of hundreds of men and women of faith. Many people running the race were tired, but the angels were handing out drinks of living water.

Hebrews 12 v 1-2

Therefore, since we are surrounded by such a huge crowd of witnesses to the life of faith, let us strip off every weight that slows us down, especially the sin that so easily hinders our progress. And let us run with endurance the race that God has set before us. We do this by keeping our eyes on Jesus, on whom our faith depends from start to finish.

Don't run the race that Satan has set before you, the round track. You'll only wear yourself out getting nowhere. Don't give the enemy the satisfaction. Come to God and repent before Him, forgive those who have hurt you, get rid of all anger and resentment. You have a choice to make and only you can make it.

Paul's final words

2 Timothy 4 v 7

I have fought a good fight, I have finished the race, and I have remained faithful. And now the prize awaits me - the crown of righteousness that the Lord, the righteous Judge, will give me on that great day of his return.

I want to finish my race and remain faithful.

HOW ABOUT YOU?

Run with Endurance the Race that God has Set Before You

ANGELS

About 15 years ago I had an encounter with angels and Jesus.

I had been badly treated by some people in the church and I was feeling rejected and very fearful. This had made me reluctant to go to church, even though I had previously enjoyed going. Many times I would set out to go; I would reach the church door but just couldn't bring myself to go in, so I went home instead.

One day, after suffering it for a year, I cried out to the Lord to help me. I heard the church bell ringing and the Lord told me start walking up the road toward church. About sixty yards from the church, I was speaking in tongues (a heavenly language given by God) as I was walking along, when I was suddenly aware that I wasn't alone, for to my left and right I saw two men dressed in white with large red crosses on their robes. Their hands were held high and they were each holding a sword. I also was aware that there were two angels behind me. In front of me was Jesus. He had shoulder length hair and I remember thinking that I mustn't walk too quickly or I would tread on His robe.

I was escorted up to the church door and taken inside. When I sat down, the angels and the Lord stood in front of me. What a way to be taken to church, with an escort of angels and Jesus! I cannot describe the peace and joy that I felt. When the service began they faded away, but I knew that spiritually they were still there. I was no longer afraid. All fear had gone and I could hardly wait for the end of the service so that I could share my experience with my close Christian friends.

The following day the Lord spoke these words to me:

"My child, I know that you have been suffering, and I have
allowed these sufferings to make you strong. I sent my
angels and I came Myself to strengthen you so that you
would have the victory in Me and give the glory to Me."

I believe the Lord was showing me that He didn't want me to
walk in fear, because He is with me in every situation. It truly
was a wonderful experience and one I shall never forget.

Many accounts of angels have been recorded around the North
Devon area.

Chapter 9

CONCLUSION

Well, that about brings me up to date with where I am right now. I've moved into a beautiful new house which the Lord found for me. God is so good - all the time! I'm completely healed of cancer. I feel a bit like Job who had more at the end of his life than the beginning. I know that the Lord has a great future planned for me - hallelujah!

I'm a more confident person now and much stronger, especially when trials come, and they do unfortunately come. My life with Jesus is absolutely wonderful and fantastic. I live each day with Him, one day at a time. That's the best way.

The word of God has always been a great source of comfort to me and I have gained my strength from the Lord's encouraging words. *His word is a lamp unto my feet.* Oh how I love Him!

I've been a Christian for 23 years and, even though I have been through many dark valleys, Jesus has always been by my side. Sometimes He's carried me when I've felt that I couldn't go on. His words of love and encouragement have sustained me and His wonderful love has overwhelmed me. I just couldn't imagine my life without Him.

I want every second to count for my Saviour for as long as I have breath in my body. My heart is to see people saved, healed and delivered. The world is full of hurting people. There is so much fear, hopelessness and despair and only one person can set you free, and His name is JESUS!

Trust yourself to God and you'll find that even in the darkest moments He will not fail you, and you will find deliverance from all your fears and anxieties. The creator of heaven and earth cares for you personally, the very hairs on your head are numbered and nothing escapes His loving eyes. He even knew you whilst you were being formed in your mother's womb, how about that!

He's a God of miracles, and remember that the power for the fulfilment of a miracle isn't in you, it's in God's promise to you. So remember, faith is what enables you to stand up to the diagnosis, scoff at the statistics, defy the prognosis and boldly announce "**I BELIEVE GOD!**"

If you want to see victory, start praising the Lord, no matter what your circumstances, for that's battle praise and when God hears it, He responds. In everything give thanks, for this is the will of God concerning you. No matter what trial you are going through, start praising the Lord and He will fill your mouth with laughter and your lips with shouts of joy even in the darkest valley. The Devil hates praise and the one thing he loves to rob you of is your joy. So whenever trouble comes your way, let it be an opportunity for joy, don't be dejected and sad *for the joy of the Lord is your strength.*

Jesus has certainly excelled Himself in my life and Oh, how I love Him and praise His wonderful name. How precious is His unfailing love to me.
Nothing living or dead, angelic or demonic, today or tomorrow, high or low, thinkable or unthinkable can ever, ever, ever separate me from the love of God.

To God be the Glory
Great things He has done,
Again and again and again.
Hallelujah!

75

Jesus, Lover of my soul
I kneel before your feet,
How can I ever thank you Lord
For making me complete.

In love and adoration
I come before your throne,
To offer up my praise to you
And worship you alone.

The fairest of ten thousand
Oh bright and morning star,
No words could ever tell you, Lord,
How wonderful you are.

Jesus you're my everything,
The rock on which I stand,
All that I have or am is yours
My life is in your hands.

Amen.

POEMS

Free from Fear

When the doctor said it was cancer
I couldn't believe what I'd heard,
I'd trusted the Lord for my healing
And stood so strong on his word.

I just couldn't speak to my Jesus
For the fear in my heart was deep,
I couldn't believe he'd allowed this
And I cried in my pillow with grief.

Then Jesus, filled with compassion,
Gently took hold of my hand,
And I cried, "Oh why has this happened,
Why, Lord? I don't understand."

He answered, "My child, you're a warrior
In the great army of your Lord,
For the time has come to banish fear
And lift high that gleaming sword.

I am taking you into dark places
Where you'll face the enemy
Riding with the King of Kings
To set the captives free."

I answered, "Oh Jesus, please help me,"
And in my time of need he was near
I will praise his name for evermore
He has freed me from all of my fear.

In my darkest hours of deep anguish
He lifted me into his arms,
And gently whispered, "Peace be still,
I am with you throughout this storm.

For I know the plans I have for you,
And I want you to understand
I'll be your strength throughout each day
For your life is in my hands."

Rise Up

Rise up, Oh mighty warrior,
And put your armour on,
You are fighting for the Lord now,
There's a battle to be won.

Don't let Satan crush you,
Your strength is in the Lord,
So arise, Oh mighty warrior,
Lift high that gleaming sword.

March forward into battle
And see the demons flee,
My anointing is upon you, child,
Beloved, you are free.

For I the Lord have healed you,
Keep on walking in my light,
And remember, my beloved,
You are precious in my sight.

Nahum Chapter 1 v 9

He will make an utter end; affliction shall not rise up a second time.

You Came Into My Life

You came into my life
And saved my soul,
Washed all my sins away
And made me whole.
Oh, how I bless your name,
Your praises sing,
I raise my hands to you,
My Sovereign King.

You touched me with your love
And gave me hope.
Through every trial, my Lord,
You helped me cope.
You healed my brokenness
And wiped my tears.
You gave me strength to face
My doubts and fears.

I'll always love you, Lord,
You are my friend,
And I know your love for me
Will never end.
My love grows deeper Lord
Each passing day,
You mean much more to me
Than words can say.

I worship you, my Lord,
Oh holy one,
You are the King of Kings
God's precious Son.
And yet you gave your life
So willingly
Two thousand years ago
On Calvary's tree.

My life, my all, I give
Set me on fire.
To serve you faithfully
Is my desire.
Oh, let me shine so bright
Like a burning flame,
That I might reach the lost
In Jesus' name.

If you're suffering at this moment, if you're really going through a difficult time and feel that there's no hope, please trust Jesus. He will be your comfort and strength. He will be the rock on which you stand. It's only in the trials and tribulations of life that your faith is tested, and if you hold on, and trust the Lord, He will bring you through and you will be a much stronger person.

Read **1 Peter Chapter 1 v 7**

Free as a Bird

I lay upon the ground
Like a bird that couldn't fly,
Wounded, hurting, all alone,
Just wanting to die.

Then you came and found me, Lord,
And rescued me from harm,
Saved me from the raging storm
And held me in your arms.

You came and filled my emptiness
With so much love and hope
When in my brokenness and fear
I could no longer cope.

You were there, Lord, you were there
Amidst my grief and fears,
You whispered words of love to me
And wiped away my tears.

Then you healed my broken wings
And I soared into the sky
On the wind of your Spirit,
Way, way up high.

High above the heavens now
I fly, I fly so free,
Filled with overflowing joy
To know that you love me.

The Father's Heart

I've seen all your pain and your sorrow,
For your cries have reached me above,
And, my child, I'll never stop trying
To pour down upon you my love.

I want you to know that I love you,
I love you so much that I died,
I know all the valleys you've been in
And, my child, it's for you that I've cried.

The joy and the peace of my presence
Are yours when you turn from your sin,
And I'll give you the keys to my kingdom,
If only you'll let me come in.

I'm here by your side gently knocking,
Behold! I stand at your door,
Just open your heart and receive me,
And my love down upon you I'll pour.

I promise that I'll never leave you,
I love you my child, can't you see,
Today is the day of salvation,
And my heart is for you to be free.

"Will you not come? Will you not come? I'm waiting for you.
See, I stand at the door and knock. If anyone hears my voice and
opens the door I will come in. I'm waiting for you right now.
I'm waiting for you to receive Me as your Saviour. I've come to
give you life. If you're bound by fear, I'll set you free.

If you're sick, I'll heal you. If you're reaching out for love, I'll put my arms around you and I'll fill you with My love. Come to Me, come to Me. I love you more than you will ever know, for I gave My life for you, I died on a cross for you, I shed My blood for you. You need Me; Oh, you need Me more than you'll ever know. Come out of the darkness into the light.

I will never leave you, never will I forsake you, never will I let you go. Just put your hands into the hands of your Saviour who loves you so much, who loves you so much, who loves you so much. Will you not come? Will you not come? I'm waiting for you; my arms are outstretched to receive you. I love you, I love you, I love you.

Your friend,
Jesus"

The above was a deep cry from the heart of God for the lost. If you don't know Jesus as your Saviour, now would be a good time to receive Him. He's coming back very soon and time is running out. Don't wait; no one knows what tomorrow may bring. Run to Him now, receive Him now and your life will never be the same again I promise you. If you truly want to know Jesus as your personal Saviour, then perhaps you would like to say the following prayer:

"Lord Jesus,

I know that You died on the cross for my sins, and I want You to be Lord of my life now and forever. Please forgive me for the many ways that I've sinned against You, and for my selfish way of living. Please, Lord Jesus, come into my life now and be my Saviour. Wash me clean, and fill me with Your Holy Spirit, and with Your help, I will learn to love and obey You as Lord of my life. Thank You for forgiving me and bringing me to God. Amen."

If you've prayed this prayer, meaning it sincerely, then God has forgiven you and made you a new person in Christ. Make sure you fellowship with other Christians.

Psalm 4 v 8

I will lie down in peace and sleep
For though I am alone, dear Lord,
You will keep me safe.
For in your tender arms I rest
Safe from every storm,
Knowing you are always there
Protecting me from harm.

Psalm 77 v 1-2

I cried out to God
Without holding back,
Oh, that he would listen to me.
When I was in trouble
I searched for the Lord
Then I found Him
And he set me free.

Psalm 40 v 12

Bend down, my Father,
And hear me I pray,
Please give me the strength
To face each new day.
Troubles surround me
Too many to count,
They've piled up so high
I can't see a way out.

I've lost all my peace
I'm sick with despair,
The burdens I carry
Are too hard to bear.
Hear my prayer, Jesus,
Please rescue me,
My heart's in a turmoil
Oh Lord, hear my plea.

Oh thank you, sweet Jesus,
That you heard my prayer,
You have lifted my burden
And showed me you care.
Now with peace in my heart
In your presence I come,
Giving glory and honour
To God's precious Son.

You are the Fairest

When I stop and think, dear Lord,
Of all you've brought me through,
I know without a single doubt
That I'm here because of you.

When I was in distress and fear
And felt there was no hope,
You held me in your loving arms
And gave me strength to cope.

I can't begin to tell you, Lord,
How much you mean to me,
I couldn't live without you now.
You are my destiny.

You are the warmth within my heart
My peace and joy each day.
I love you, Lord, I love you, Lord,
Much more than words can say.

You are the fairest of them all
Your words are filled with grace,
No one in heaven or on the earth
Could ever take your place.

The Lord gave me the following poem when I was going through a very difficult time. I was broken, hurt and weary, and my heart was heavy. I came before the Lord and waited in His presence. He then gave me the following poem called "Take me to the River.You know, problems will come, that's inevitable, but there's no better place to be than in the river of God just allowing His Holy Spirit to fill and refresh you. Jesus says in His Word, *"Come to me all of you who are weary and carry heavy burdens, and I will give you rest."*

Take me to the River

Weary, heavy laden,
I come to be refreshed,
Take me to the river
Where I know I will be blessed.

Deep into the river, Lord,
How I long to be set free,
To feel your love and tenderness
Washing over me.

Let your healing waters
Cleanse me, Lord, anew,
Take me to the river
For my only hope is you.

Deep now in the river
No more am I alone,
Oh, such love and joy and peace
Is flowing from your throne.

Come to Me

"Are you weak and heavy laden?
Then I will give you rest,
Come deep into my river,
Come and be refreshed.

You have carried many burdens
And I've seen the tears you've cried,
But remember, my beloved,
I'm right there by your side.

My hands are there to hold you,
I will never let you go,
Come, my child, and be set free,
And let my river flow.

Nowhere will you find such peace
Or healing for your soul,
And as the water covers you
I, the Lord, will make you whole."

"Come to Me, My weary one. Come into the river of My love, joy and peace. Come and be refreshed. Let My living waters wash over you. Come, come now, for I am here and I am holding out My hand to you. Take it and step into the river. Hold fast for you shall find rest and peace and I will restore and heal you, for I am the Lord your God. Come, come unto Me, you who are weary and heavy laden and I will give you rest. Let My waters wash over you for nowhere will you find such refreshing and peace. I'm calling you, beloved, and I am waiting for you to come."

The Lord is my rock, my fortress and my Saviour. My God is my rock in whom I find protection. He is my shield, the strength of my salvation and my stronghold and His banner over me is love.

My Refuge

He is my refuge and my strength,
I have no need to fear,
In darkness or temptation
My God is always near.

He guides me through the storms of life
And gently takes my hand,
In the deepest darkest valley
Jesus gives me strength to stand.

He is my fortress and my shield,
He's watching over me,
And if I put my trust in him,
I'll walk in victory.

Secure and safe within his care
He watches from above,
He knows the very path I take
For His banner over me is love.

The following words were given to me by the Lord when I was going through a very difficult time.

Do not Worry

Do not worry, do not fear,
I am with you, I am near,
Trust me for your needs each day
Take my hand, I'll lead the way.

And when problems cause you pain
I can help you smile again,
I will share your falling tears
Wipe your eyes and hold you near.

Keep on walking in my light
You are precious in my sight,
I will never let you go
For, my child, I love you so.